Red As a Fire Truck

written by **Molly Dingles**

illustrated by **Walter Velez**

dingles & company New Jersey

First printing

PUBLISHED BY dingles&company
P.O. Box 508 • Sea Girt, New Jersey • 08750
WEBSITE: www.dingles.com • E-MAIL: info@dingles.com

LIBRARY BINDING EDITION DISTRIBUTED BY **GUMDROP BOOKS**
P.O. Box 505 • Bethany, Missouri • 64424
(660) 425-7777

Library of Congress Catalog Card No.: 2002141511
ISBN: 1-891997-19-X

Printed in the United States of America

●

ART DIRECTED & DESIGNED BY Barbie Lambert
EDITED BY Andrea Curley / EDITORIAL ASSISTANT Allison Bolte

DEVELOPMENT TEAM
Kathleen P. Miller, Meredith Paril,
Leslie Greenley

For Rocky

Molly Dingles

is the author of *Jinka Jinka Jelly Bean* and *Little Lee Lee's Birthday Bang*. As Judy Zocchi, she has written the *Paulie & Sasha* series. She is a writer and lyricist who holds a bachelor's degree in fine arts/theater from Mount Saint Mary's College and a master's degree in educational theater from New York University. She lives in Manasquan, New Jersey, with her husband, David.

Walter Velez

was born in New York. He attended the High School of Art and Design and later the School of Visual Arts. He has done illustration work for many major book and gaming companies. He is known for the popular series *Thieves World* as well as the *Myth* series for Ace Books. He has also produced trading cards for *Goosebumps* and *Dune*. In addition, Walter has illustrated several *Star Wars* books for Random House. He lives in Queens, New York, with his wife, Kriti, and daughter, Kassandra.

community of color series

The **Community of Color** series is more than just a series of books about colors. The series demonstrates how individual people, places, and things combine to form a community. It allows children to view the world in segments and then experience the wonderment and value of the community as a whole.

Red as an apple

Red as a rose

Red as a lollipop

Red as a nose.

Red as a cherry

Red as a ladybug

Red as a light.

Red as a wagon

Red as a dart

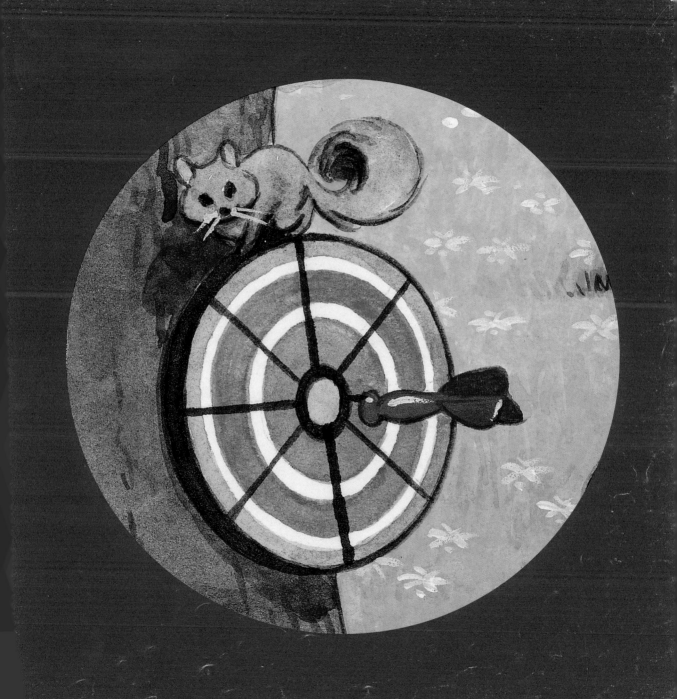

Red as a fire truck

Red as a heart.

The color Red is all around.

ABOUT COLOR

Use the Community of Color series to teach your child to identify the most basic colors and to help him or her relate these colors to objects in the real world. ASK:

- What color is this book about?
- Can you name all the red things in this park scene?
- How many red apples can you find?
- What red toys are there in this picture?

ABOUT COMMUNITY

Use the Community of Color series to teach your child how he or she is an important part of the community. EXPLAIN TO YOUR CHILD WHAT A COMMUNITY IS:

- A community is a place where people live, work, and play together.
- Your family is a community.
- Your school is a community.
- Your neighborhood is a community.
- The world is one big community.

Everyone plays an important part in making a community work - moms, dads, boys, girls, police officers, firefighters, teachers, mail carriers, garbage collectors, store clerks, and even animals are all important parts of a community. USE THESE QUESTIONS TO FURTHER THE CONVERSATION:

- How are the people in the park interacting with one another?
- How are the people different from one another? How are they the same?
- What do they have in common?
- How is the community you see in this book like your community? How is it different?
- Describe your community.

ABOUT FEELINGS

Colors can describe as well as evoke different emotions. Encourage your child to describe the feelings that the color red inspires. ASK:

- How does the color make you feel?
- Name your favorite red thing in this book. Why is it your favorite?
- Name your favorite red thing at home. Why is it your favorite?
- Can you tell how the people in the picture feel by looking at their faces? Do you ever feel the same way? When? Why?

TRY SOMETHING NEW . . . Lend a hand! Help your local firefighters wash a fire truck (but get permission before you do).

community of color series